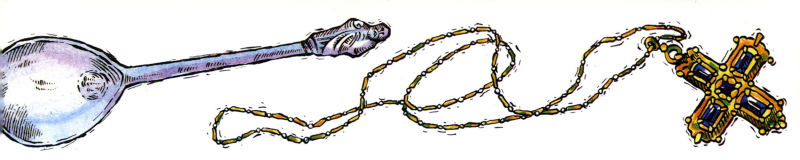

THE FACTS ABOUT

THE TUDORS AND STUARTS

Dereen Taylor

WAYLAND

First published in Great Britain in 1994 by Simon and Schuster Young Books
Reprinted by Macdonald Young Books in 1997 as *What Do We Know About the Tudors and Stuarts?* by Richard Tames
This differentiated text version by Dereen Taylor, published in 2005 by Hodder Wayland, an imprint of Hodder Children's Books

This paperback edition published in 2007 by Wayland, an imprint of Hachette Children's Books

Hachette Children's Books
338 Euston Road
London NW1 3BH

Original series design: Dave West
Designer and illustrator: Celia Hart
Layout for this edition: Jane Hawkins
Editor for this edition: Hayley Leach

Photograph acknowledgements: The Bridgeman Art Library: cover, p23(b) (Christy's), p26(r) (V&A Museum), p28(1) Bible Society, London), p29(b) (British Library), p33(b), p34(1) (V&A Museum); British Library, p14(b), p25(b), p43(tr); Christ's Hospital, Horsham, p20(r); Devonshire Collection, Chatsworth, reproduced by permission of the Chatsworth Settlement Trustees, p37(t); E.T. Archive, endpapers, p8(t) (V&A Museum), p9, p12(1), p14(t) (Marquess of Bath), p22(b) (V&A Museum), p24(t) (Museum of London); The Earl of Rosebery/Scottish National Portrait Gallery, p33(t); English Heritage Photo Library, p18(b), p43(tl); Mary Evans Picture Library, p29(t), p31; John Freeman, p35(1); reproduces by kind permission of the Trustees of the Geffrye Museum Trust Ltd, p27(b), p36(r); Glasgow University Library, p30(t); Hulton Deutsch Collection, p20(1); reproduced by the permission of the Marquess of Bath, Longleat House, Warminster, Wiltshire, p18(t); The Museum of the History of Science, University of Oxford, p38; Museum of London, p15, p21, p37(b); National Maritime Museum, p40; National Portrait Gallery, London, p17(1), p26(1), p32 p36(1); The National Trust Photographic Library, p28(r) (Matthew Antrobus), p35(r); Picturepoint, p27(t) (Museum of London), p43(b); Plimoth Plantation, Inc., Plymouth, Massachusetts USA (John Ulven), p41(b); The Science Museum, p23(t), p30(b), p39(t); Richard Tames, p41(t); Tate Gallery, London, p16; Thomas Photos, Oxford, p39(b); TRIP, p8(b) (Bob Turner), p19 (R. Styles), p34(r) (J. Watters); by courtesy of the Board of Trustees of the Victoria and Albert Museum, p12(r), p24(b), p25(t); Woodmansterne Picture Library, p17(r), p22(t) (Castle Museum, York).

Picture Research: Valerie Mulcahy

Printed in China

British Library Cataloguing in Publication Data
Taylor, Dereen
The facts about the Tudors and Stuarts
  1.Great Britain – Civilization – 16th century – Juvenile literature 2.Great Britain – History – Tudors, 1485-1603 – Juvenile literature
  Title
  942'.05

ISBN-10: 0 7502 5102 6
ISBN-13: 978 0 7502 5102 0

Endpapers: This cushion cover dating from the late 1500s depicts a hunting and hawking scene richly embroidered in silk and silver thread.

CONTENTS

Words that appear in **bold** can be found in the glossary on page 44.

WHO WERE THE TUDORS AND STUARTS?

Tudor and Stuart are the family names of the Kings and Queens who ruled Britain between 1485 and 1714. About two million people lived in England around the year 1500. By 1700, this had gone up to five million people. The number of people living in Scotland, Ireland and Wales doubled from just over one million to just over two million. Only about one in ten of these people lived in cities.

◄ ARMADA JEWEL

This jewel shows a picture of Elizabeth I. It was made to celebrate the defeat of the Spanish Armada in 1588.

SCOTLAND

St Andrew's flag

Union flag of 1603

IRELAND

ENGLAND

WALES

St George's flag

ORDINARY PEOPLE ▼

The photograph below shows how ordinary people would have looked in Elizabethan times. Ordinary people had no say in how the country was run. They had to obey God and their monarch.

THE UNION OF 1603 ▲

From the 1530s onwards, Wales and England were ruled as one country. When Elizabeth I died in 1603, James VI of Scotland became King. The Stuarts ruled England and Scotland as separate countries.

◄ DYING FOR RELIGIOUS BELIEFS

Quarrels over religion led to the killings of both Protestants and Catholics. This famous woodcut shows two Protestant Bishops being burned in Oxford in 1555. They were killed because they refused to give up the Protestant faith.

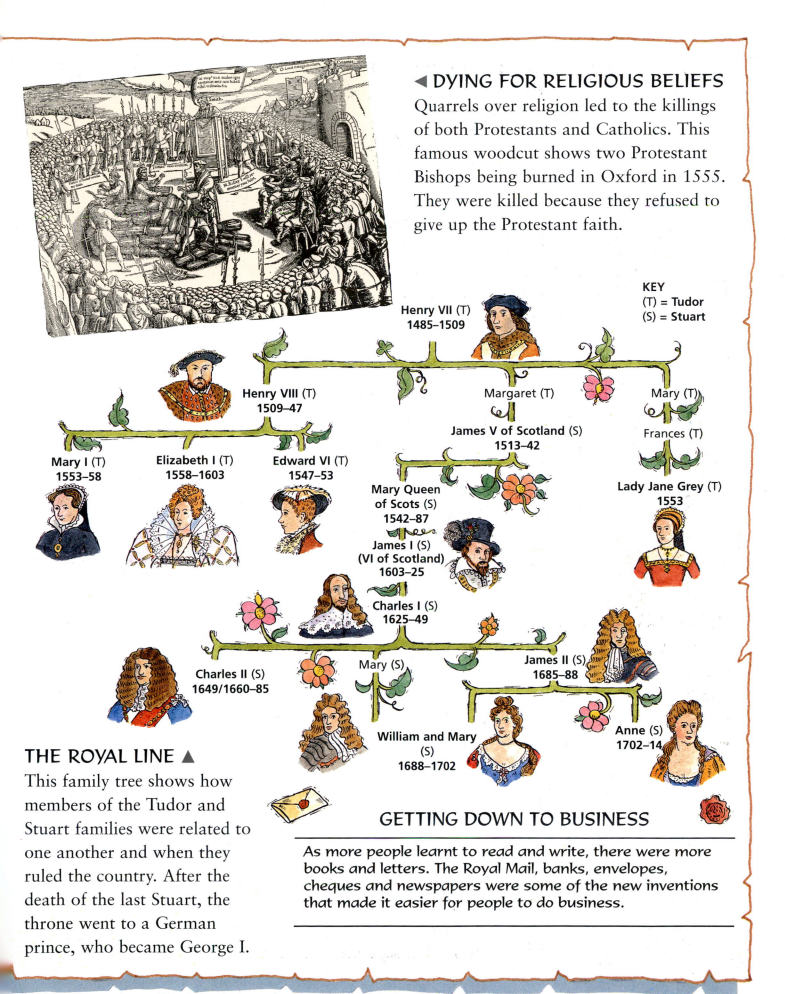

KEY
(T) = Tudor
(S) = Stuart

Henry VII (T)
1485–1509

Henry VIII (T)
1509–47

Margaret (T)

Mary (T)

James V of Scotland (S)
1513–42

Frances (T)

Mary I (T)
1553–58

Elizabeth I (T)
1558–1603

Edward VI (T)
1547–53

Mary Queen
of Scots (S)
1542–87

Lady Jane Grey (T)
1553

James I (S)
(VI of Scotland)
1603–25

Charles I (S)
1625–49

Charles II (S)
1649/1660–85

Mary (S)

James II (S)
1685–88

William and Mary
(S)
1688–1702

Anne (S)
1702–14

THE ROYAL LINE ▲

This family tree shows how members of the Tudor and Stuart families were related to one another and when they ruled the country. After the death of the last Stuart, the throne went to a German prince, who became George I.

GETTING DOWN TO BUSINESS

As more people learnt to read and write, there were more books and letters. The Royal Mail, banks, envelopes, cheques and newspapers were some of the new inventions that made it easier for people to do business.

TIMELINE

	HENRY VII 1485–1509	HENRY VIII 1509–1547	EDWARD VI 1547–1553	MARY 1553–1558	ELIZABETH I 1558–1603	JAMES I 1603–1625	CHARLES I 1625–1649
ENGLAND AND WALES	Beginning of central government. **Tudor rose**	Henry declares himself Head of the Church of England, 1534. Closing of monasteries begins. Union of England and Wales.	Protestants gain control of church. **Bible**	Roman Catholics persecute Protestants.	Protestants persecute Roman Catholics. Sir Francis Drake sails round the world, 1577–80. Defeat of the Spanish Armada, 1588.	Catholic 'Gunpowder Plot' to blow-up King and Parliament, 1605. Authorised translation of the Bible, 1611.	Struggle for power between King and Parliament. 100,000 people killed in **civil wars** (1642–49). Charles I executed, 1649.
SCOTLAND AND IRELAND	**Cannon**	English defeat Scots at Battle of Flodden, 1513.	English defeat Scots at Pinkie, 1547.	**Coin**	John Knox leads Protestants in Scotland. **Execution** of Mary, Queen of Scots, 1587.	James rules England and Scotland as separate kingdoms. Protestants begin to settle in Ulster.	Scottish fight against unfair rule of monarch and invade England.
REST OF EUROPE	Spread of printing means cheap books. Muslims expelled from Spain.	Martin Luther begins Protestant movement against Catholic Church. Ottoman Turks conquer Hungary.	England gives up Boulogne to France. Michelangelo becomes chief **architect** of St Peter's in Rome, 1547.	Philip II of Spain (1556–98) rules huge European-American empire. England gives up Calais in France, 1558.	Religious wars in France. **Star-shaped fort**	Thirty Years War (1618–48) in Central Europe.	Power restored to **monarch** in France.
REST OF WORLD	Columbus reaches West Indies. Portuguese reach India.	Magellan sails round the world, 1519–22. French begin to explore Canada. Ivan the Terrible doubles the size of the Russian empire.	**Clay pipe** Jesuit **missionaries** reach South America.	Richard Chancellor travels to Russia via the Arctic, 1553–54.	Tobacco introduced to Europe from America. Akbar expands Mughal Empire in India.	English and Dutch increase trading with Asia. English settle in Virginia and New England, America. French find Quebec in Canada.	Taj Mahal built, 1632–54.

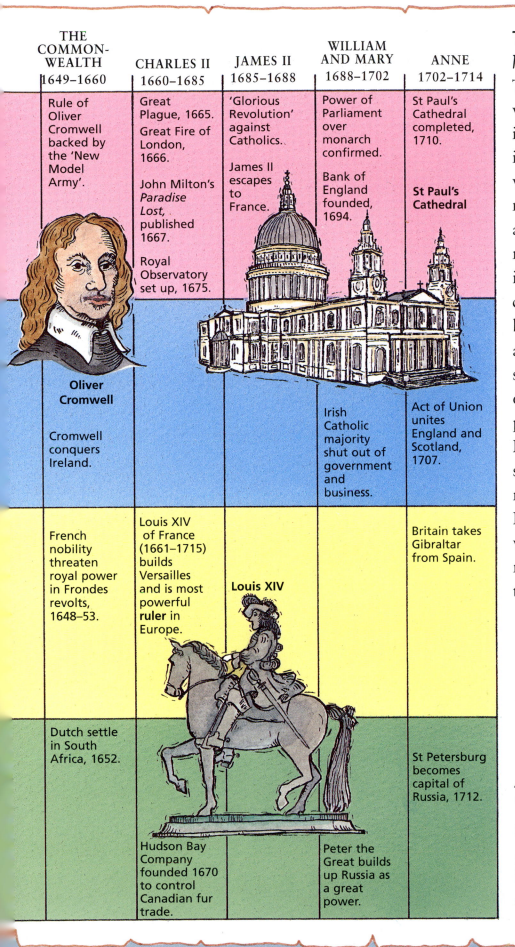

THE COMMON-WEALTH 1649–1660	CHARLES II 1660–1685	JAMES II 1685–1688	WILLIAM AND MARY 1688–1702	ANNE 1702–1714
Rule of Oliver Cromwell backed by the 'New Model Army'.	Great Plague, 1665. Great Fire of London, 1666. John Milton's *Paradise Lost*, published 1667. Royal Observatory set up, 1675.	'Glorious Revolution' against Catholics. James II escapes to France.	Power of Parliament over monarch confirmed. Bank of England founded, 1694.	St Paul's Cathedral completed, 1710. **St Paul's Cathedral**
Oliver Cromwell Cromwell conquers Ireland.			Irish Catholic majority shut out of government and business.	Act of Union unites England and Scotland, 1707.
French nobility threaten royal power in Frondes revolts, 1648–53.	Louis XIV of France (1661–1715) builds Versailles and is most powerful **ruler** in Europe.	**Louis XIV**		Britain takes Gibraltar from Spain.
Dutch settle in South Africa, 1652.	Hudson Bay Company founded 1670 to control Canadian fur trade.		Peter the Great builds up Russia as a great power.	St Petersburg becomes capital of Russia, 1712.

THE POWER OF THE MONARCH

This timeline shows who was on the throne when important events took place in Britain and around the world. Kings and Queens made all the big decisions about war, politics and religion. The royal court also influenced fashions in clothes, food, music and buildings. In most of Europe at this time, rulers became stronger and took less notice of courts, councils or parliaments. But in Britain Parliament actually got stronger. Charles I tried to rule without Parliament. Parliament even tried to rule without a King. In the end, ruler and Parliament learned to work together.

A WIDER WORLD

There was an increase in trading by sea with America, Asia and Africa. This was an important change for Britain and the whole of Europe.

WHERE DID PEOPLE GET THEIR FOOD?

Growing food was the most common kind of work. Men worked in fields. Women kept hens, milked cows and made butter and cheese. Even children helped out. Most food was sold at local markets. In 1700, London had 30 markets selling food or livestock.

CHILDREN AT WORK ▼

This tapestry shows children gathering grapes to make wine. Most wine was **imported** from Europe, but it was warm enough to grow some grapes in the south of England.

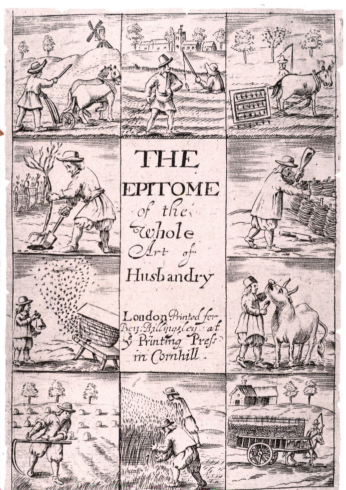

▲ FARMING

The invention of printing meant cheap books on farming were available to more people. You can see from this book cover that all the tools and equipment were simple and could be made on the farm or by the village blacksmith.

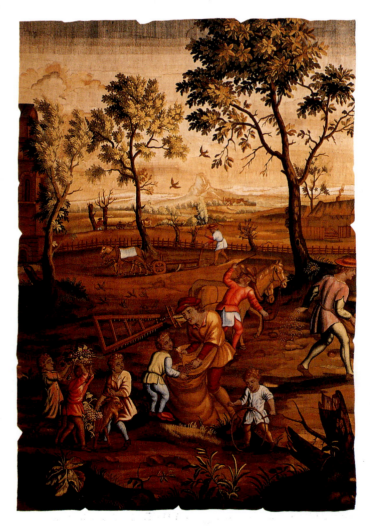

BREWING ▼

People drank ale because it often contained fewer germs than water. Even children drank it. Many people brewed their own beer using simple tools like the ones below. In Stuart times, one-seventh of all the money spent in England went on beer!

Funnel

Mash-stick

Mash-stirrer

Tools for brewing

Tea, coffee and chocolate arrived in Britain after 1650 but only the rich could afford to buy them.

Most people refused to eat tomatoes or potatoes because they thought they were poisonous!

Turkeys and geese were marched 200 kilometres from Norfolk to London for people in London to eat.

HERBS ▼

Even in towns people grew herbs. They were used to flavour soups and to make medicines, soap and make-up.

Mint

Thyme

Rosemary

BRITAIN

EUROPE

NORTH AMERICA

maize

pineapples

turkeys

CANARY ISLANDS

bananas

AFRICA

CHINA

INDIA

tea

pepper

INDONESIA

chocolate

coconut

coffee

tomatoes

SOUTH AMERICA

potatoes

spices

AUSTRALIA

▲ FOOD FROM OTHER COUNTRIES

Countries in Europe began to trade more with America, Asia and Africa. Different foods from these far-away countries were introduced to people in Europe. Some, like potatoes, could be grown in Europe. But tea and some spices had to be brought on long journeys by ships from the hot countries where they grew. It usually took six weeks to bring sugar from the West Indies and four months to get cloves or nutmeg from Indonesia.

DID PEOPLE EAT WELL?

BANQUETS ▼

This painting of the Cobham children shows how well the rich ate around 1550. The children are finishing their meal with fresh fruit and even have enough left over to feed their pets!

An ordinary family spent four-fifths of their money on food. Many servants and labourers were partly paid with food. Poor people grew vegetables and kept pigs for pork and bacon. Villages often had common land where people grazed cows and gathered berries. Wealthy people sometimes ate too much red meat and rich wine and not enough vegetables. This gave them stomach problems and skin complaints.

◄ EVERYDAY MEALS

This picture shows a much poorer family. They are eating soup with bread. The youngest children have no chairs to sit on while they eat. Few people ate breakfast. The main meal of the day was at noon. Honey was used to sweeten foods instead of sugar.

TABLEWARE ▼

Decorated wooden plates called *trenchers*, were used for serving sticky sweets. Rich people began to use coffee pots and cups like these.

Trencher

Coffee pot

Silver cup

THE PARR POT ▼

This beautiful pot was made around 1500. It was used at banquets for drinking fine wines from France, Spain and Germany.

RECIPE ▼

Printing made recipe books more common. This is a recipe for stewing sparrows. A pottle is about 2.3 litres of liquid. Sippets are cubes of toasted bread. Seething is boiling.

> Take good ale a pottle and set it over the fire to boil, and put in your sparrows and scum the broth, then put therein onions, parsley, thyme, rosemary chopped small, pepper and saffron, with cloves and mace. And make sippets and lay the sparrows upon with the said broth and in the seething put in a piece of sweet butter if need be.

Tudor people used lots of herbs and spices in their cooking. They must have liked food to have a very strong flavour.

🍷 EATING WELL 🍽

In 1508, the Duke of Buckingham gave a feast for 459 people. The menu included swans, heron, larks and peacocks. There were 678 loaves, 259 bottles of ale, 400 eggs, 200 oysters, twelve sheep, ten pigs and two calves. The total cost was £7. This was more money than a farm labourer earned in a year.

In Tudor times, if the harvest failed, up to half the population (about 2,500,000 people) might go hungry or even starve to death.

DID THEY HAVE FAMILIES LIKE OURS?

Diseases like measles or influenza could kill you in Tudor and Stuart times. You could even die from a bad cut if it became infected. Many women died having babies and about one child in five died before their first birthday. Often children left home when they were ten years old to become apprentices. They lived with their master's family. Only beggars and old people with no one to care for them lived alone.

THE SALTONSTALL FAMILY ▼

This painting shows Sir Richard Saltonstall and his family. In the bed is his first wife who had died. Dead relatives were often painted in family portraits.

In 1550, Sir William Petre, who worked for Elizabeth I, had 21 servants at his main home. He had another 12 servants at his London house. The wage bill at the hall was £51 a year. There were extra costs for the servants' uniforms and food. The mother of a wealthy family had to make sure the servants were doing their work properly. Good servants were looked after even when they were old and couldn't work anymore.

A BANQUET SCENE ▲

This is part of a painting telling the life story of Sir Henry Unton. Sir Henry is sitting third from the left at the table. Entertaining guests was a big family occasion.

Windmill

Kite

Spinning-top and whip

◄▲ TOYS AND GAMES

Young children played with dolls, marbles, drums, kites and spinning-tops. Older boys were taken hunting while girls did needlework.

▲ BRINGING UP BABY

This high-chair and the two dolls would have belonged to the baby of a wealthy family. The baby might also have had a solid silver rattle.

DID PEOPLE LIVE IN HOUSES?

Most people built their houses from materials they could find nearby. If there was no stone, they used wooden frames filled in with mud or brick. The strong rule of the Tudors meant that houses no longer needed thick walls and moats to protect them from invaders. Architects like Inigo Jones and Christopher Wren began to replace the master-mason as designers of houses.

BIG HOUSES ▶

This is a picture of Longleat in Wiltshire. It was built 1560–80 for Sir John Thynne. Its design was based on new ideas from Italy. Great houses had a long gallery where family portraits could be hung. Even the homes of the rich were draughty. Heating came from open fires of wood or coal. Screens and curtains were used to keep out the cold.

◀ INTERIORS

This picture on the left shows the hall of a great house around 1600. Carpet is used to cover the table instead of the floor! People sat on benches instead of chairs. The only heat comes from one big fireplace. The introduction of glass windows meant that rooms were much lighter.

YEOMAN'S HOUSE ▶

This yeoman's home had luxuries like glass windows, chimneys and a tile roof. Even so, the **servants** may have slept on a straw mattress in the kitchen.

◀ FURNITURE

A local joiner usually made furniture. Oak was often used, as it was a solid wood that lasted for many years. When chairs with padded seats came in around 1650, only wealthy homes had them. Most people sat on stools or benches.

Upholstered chair

A POOR FAMILY'S HOVEL ▼

Poor people's homes had thatched roofs and windows with wooden shutters. Some had a loft for sleeping in and storing food.

NEW THINGS IN THE HOME

First record of carpets in England.	1482
First conservatory built in England.	1562
First piped water supply to private houses.	1582
First water closet (toilet) put into the home of Sir John Harington at Kelston, in Bath.	1589
First greenhouse built at Oxford.	1621
Wallpaper begins to come into use.	1690s

◀ ANIMALS IN THE HOME

Poor people kept cows and horses indoors in winter to shelter them. Keeping animals indoors helped to keep the house warm.

Hovel

DID BOYS AND GIRLS GO TO SCHOOL?

The village priest taught children about religion and how to read and write. But many priests were too lazy to do a good job. Also, poor people thought it was more important to be earning money rather than learning. Children from wealthy families were often taught at home by a tutor. Both rich and poor families thought education was only important for boys. Girls learned cooking and sewing.

▲ SCHOOL

This woodcut from about 1580 shows a Tudor grammar school. Everyone is being taught in the same room. Older pupils helped by teaching lessons to the younger ones. As you can see, boys were beaten for not doing their work properly. Most of the day was spent learning Latin. Latin was a language understood by educated people all over Europe. Can you see the music on the wall? Singing was a very popular activity.

SCHOOL UNIFORM ▼

This modern photograph shows the uniform of a school called Christ's Hospital, founded by Edward VI in 1553.

TUDOR EDUCATION STANDARDS

In London around 1600, about three people out of every four could read and write. This figure was as low as one out of three people in other parts of the country. Schoolmasters were paid poorly and often were not very well educated themselves. School hours were very long and there were prayers before and after lessons. Some schools had scholarships for very clever boys, but hardly ever for girls. Poor pupils were sometimes given lessons in return for cleaning classrooms.

Stylus

Quill pen

Knife

Ink pot

HORNBOOK ▲

This hornbook was made from wood and covered with a thin layer of animal horn to protect the letters from being rubbed off. Young children often used a hornbook to learn the alphabet.

WRITING ▲

Children learnt to write on a slate with chalk. The chalk could be wiped off and the slate used again and again. Writing was usually done with a feather pen called a quill pen. A sharp knife was used to keep the point of the quill pen sharp. Ink could be made at home, using soot from the chimney. Pencils were invented in Tudor times, but were not very common until around 1800. Paper, made from rags, was very expensive. A lot of people could only scribble their name, rather than write a whole letter.

WHO WENT TO WORK IN TUDOR AND STUART TIMES?

Most landowners were wealthy enough not to have to work. Many boys learned skilled trades by doing an apprenticeship with a master-craftsman

for seven years. A legal agreement was made between the apprentice's parents and the master-craftsman. It was rare for girls to be given an apprenticeship.

◀ TEXTILES

Farming was the nation's biggest industry. Making cloth out of wool or linen was the second biggest industry. As this museum reconstruction shows, most weavers worked at home. Making a 'broadcloth', 11 metres long by 2 metres wide, kept 15 people in work for one week.

EMBROIDERY ▶

Wealthy men and women liked to wear embroidered clothes like this beautiful glove. Rich women did embroidery as a hobby.

Poor women embroidered as a way of working at home to be with their children.

SHIPBUILDING

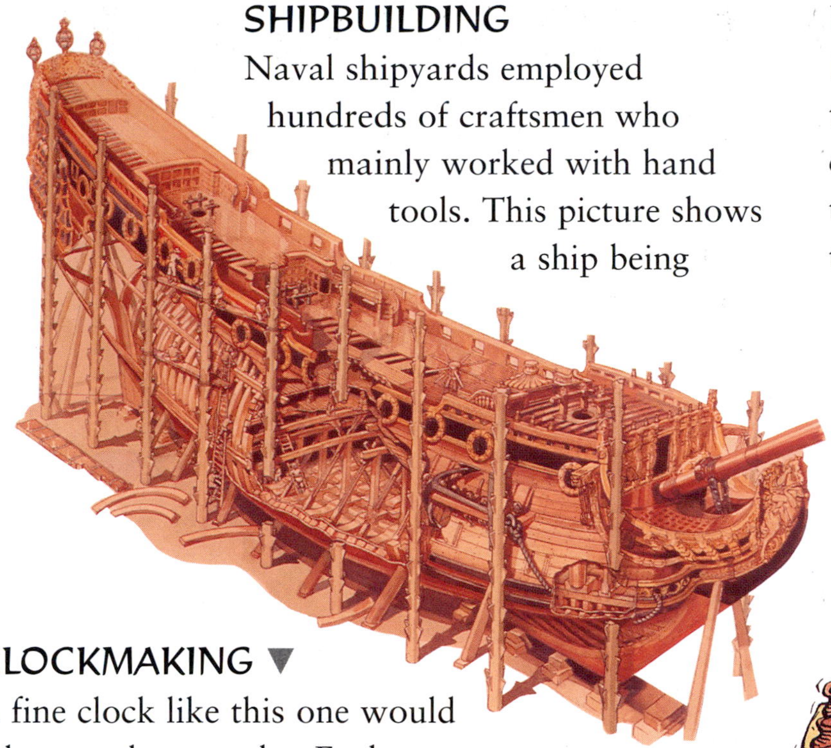

Naval shipyards employed hundreds of craftsmen who mainly worked with hand tools. This picture shows a ship being built for the Royal Navy around 1680. Can you see the holes for the guns? In 1600, the average cargo ship weighed about 60 tonnes. This had gone up to 300 tonnes by 1700.

POTTERY ▼

Potters made jugs and bowls to use for cooking and eating. They also made large jars for storing oil and wine. Potters began to copy the beautiful style of pottery **imported** from China.

CLOCKMAKING ▼

A fine clock like this one would take months to make. Each part was individually crafted by hand. During the 1600s, clocks became more accurate at telling the time.

Potter's wheel and pots

NEW OCCUPATIONS

Many people found work mining raw materials such as coal, iron, tin, copper and lead. Other people were employed to make glass, paper and guns. As interest in science grew, London became a leading centre for making telescopes and barometers.

WHAT DID PEOPLE DO IN THEIR SPARE TIME?

In 1616, the people of Lancashire complained to James I that Puritans were trying to stop their usual Sunday amusements. The King took the side of the people and gave permission for dancing, archery, athletics, morris dancing and Maypoles. But he said bowling and the baiting of bears and bulls were not allowed on a Sunday.

FROST FAIR ▲

The River Thames was broader and shallower in Tudor times. It flowed more slowly and in very cold winters it could freeze solid. This picture shows a fair on a frozen river with entertainers and sideshows during the winter of 1683–1684.

▲ VIRGINALS

These virginals belonged to Queen Elizabeth I. They were a kind of early piano. Music was a popular pastime for both rich and poor people.

HUNTING ▶

Hunting was important in Tudor and Stuart times. It was training for war and provided meat for the family. This carpet scene shows a horseman with a spear charging a wild pig. Two more hunters have guns for shooting birds. Can you see a man catching a fish? Gloves and hoods (below right) were used when hunting with birds of prey.

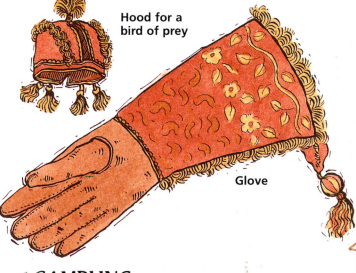

Hood for a bird of prey

Glove

◀ GAMBLING

This book cover (left) shows billiards, backgammon, dice, cards and cock-fighting. These were popular gambling games around 1680.

NEW ENTERTAINMENTS

Workers who came over from Holland introduced skating on frozen canals to the English and golf to the Scottish. Hockey was being played in Ireland in 1527. Charles II made Newmarket a great centre for horse racing. Coffee houses also became popular while he was King.

WHAT DID TUDOR AND STUART PEOPLE WEAR?

The wonderful portraits of Tudor and Stuart times show rich people trying to look their best. They showed off their wealth by wearing

furs and feathers, and clothes made from expensive cloths like silk and velvet. Ordinary people had to stick to hard-wearing clothes made of home-made materials, such as wool, linen and leather. These clothes were rarely washed and were usually worn until they fell apart!

▲ LADY JANE GREY

This portrait shows Lady Jane Grey wearing a dress lined with ermine, a very expensive fur. The red underskirt is embroidered with gold braid and pearls.

RICHARD SACKVILLE, EARL OF DORSET ▲

This painting of the Earl of Dorset shows the fashion for men's clothes around 1610. His breeches are stuffed to make them stand out from his waist. His armour is included in the picture to show he is a soldier.

◀ SHOES

In 1650, fashionable men wore high-heeled shoes. These fine leather shoes were probably worn indoors. Outdoors, men wore high leather boots and women wore wooden platform shoes, called pattens, over their dainty silk slippers.

Necklaces

Rings

Earrings

JEWELLERY ▲

Men as well as women wore rings, chains and earrings. Sir Walter Raleigh paid £30 for a decorated hatband. This was enough to buy uniforms for seven army officers, plus two pairs of shoes each!

◀ NO FASHION FOR MOST

Most poor people had only one or two changes of clothes. This man (left) is selling second-hand clothes in the street.

HAIRSTYLES ✂

Hair was rarely washed but often oiled or curled. Ladies also used lace, ribbons and flowers to decorate their hair.

In the 1660s, men wore long wigs made of horsehair.

WAS RELIGION IMPORTANT?

Throughout Europe the Protestants challenged the power of the Roman Catholic Church. Protestants wanted people to be able to read the Bible for themselves and make up their own minds about what they believed. Britain's rulers also tried to control what people believed. But many Catholics and Protestants were prepared to die rather than give up their beliefs. As well as a deep belief in religion there was also a widespread belief in magic and witchcraft.

FOUNTAINS ABBEY ▶

In the 1530s, Henry VIII took over the lands owned by the church and closed down the monasteries. This photograph (right) shows what happened to Fountains Abbey in Yorkshire when people took wood, lead, glass and stone from its buildings.

◀ THE BIBLE IN ENGLISH

By the 1540s, Bibles like this one (left) were in English, not Latin. The 1611 'King James Bible' is the version still used today.

 BEST SELLERS

The most popular books of this period were about religion. Foxe's 'Book of Martyrs' (1563) is about people who had died for the Protestant faith. Milton's poem 'Paradise Lost' (1667) is about the devil.

ROMAN CATHOLICS ▼

Mary, Queen of Scots carried a Catholic prayer book and **rosary** beads at her **execution** in 1587. After Britain became Protestant, Catholics were banned from being MPs, judges or army officers. This lasted until 1829.

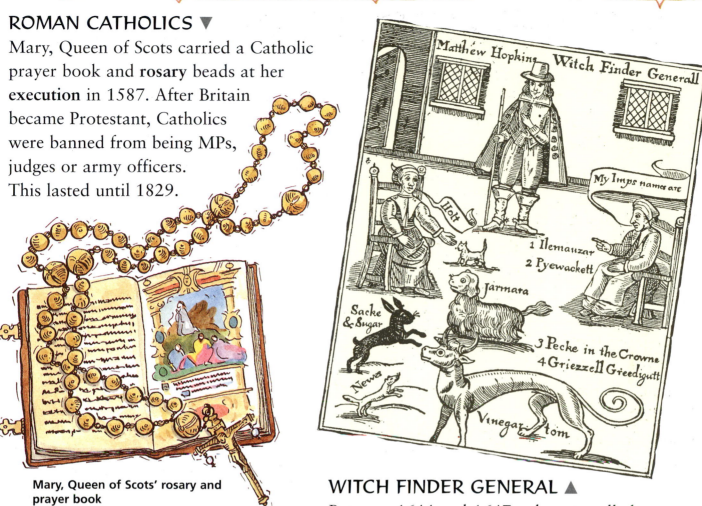

Mary, Queen of Scots' rosary and prayer book

WITCH FINDER GENERAL ▲

Between 1644 and 1647, a lawyer called Matthew Hopkins sent 230 people to their death because they were thought to be witches. Then he, too, was hanged as a witch.

◄ QUAKERS

George Fox founded the Society of Friends in the 1640s. Another name for the society was the 'Quakers'. They allowed anyone to speak at their meetings, including women, as you can see in this picture.

DID TUDOR AND STUART PEOPLE GO THE DOCTOR?

There were two kinds of doctor – physicians and barber-surgeons. The physicians were well educated and knew that diet and rest were important for curing many illnesses. Barber-surgeons treated broken bones and battle wounds. They also cut hair. A favourite cure for many illnesses was to bleed people by opening a vein or putting leeches on their skin. Poor people went to 'wise women' who made medicines from herbs.

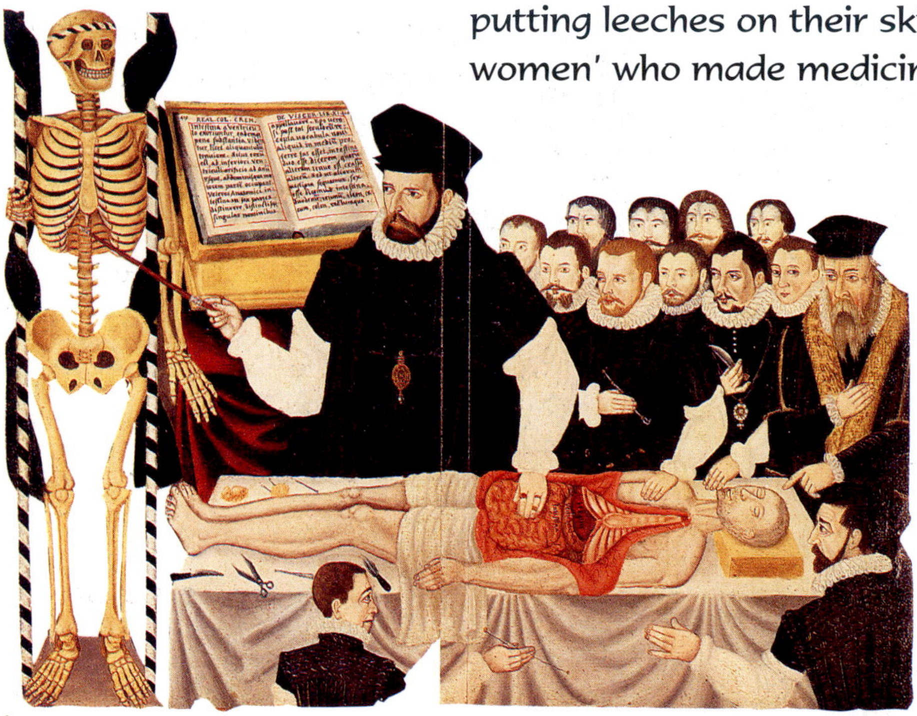

◀ **BARBER-SURGEONS**

This picture (left) shows a lecture at the Barber-Surgeons' Hall in 1581. Below are some of the tools surgeons used for **amputations**. There were no painkillers or **antiseptics** and patients often died from shock or infection.

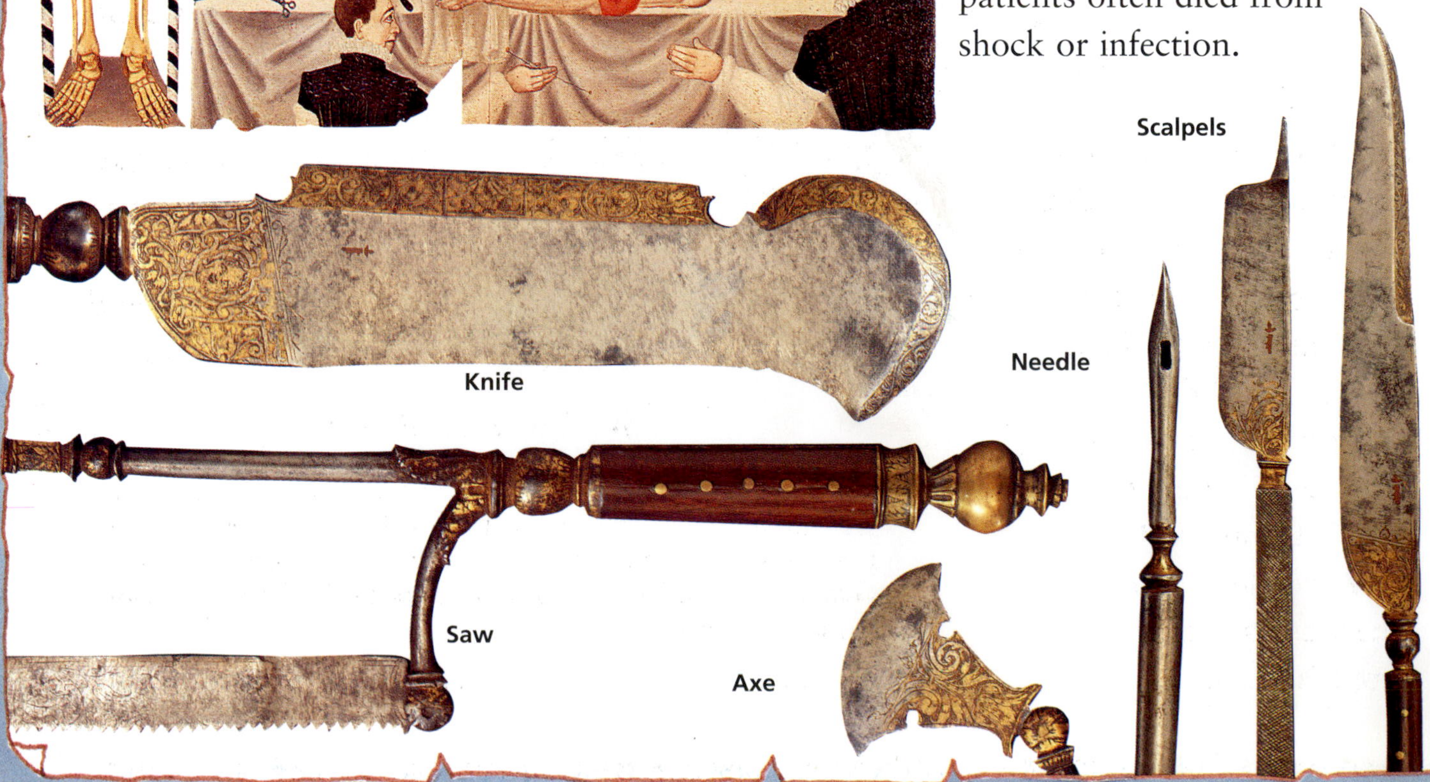

Scalpels

Needle

Knife

Saw

Axe

Mortar

Pestle

Rue

Angelica

MOVING OUT OF TOWN ▲

The woodcut above shows people running away from an outbreak of plague in a town. Can you see the town gateway? Doctors didn't know how to treat the plague. If you had it, you were locked up in your house for 40 days to stop you spreading it to other people.

THE PLAGUE

There were major outbreaks of plague throughout this period. The Great Plague of 1665 killed 100,000 people. Plague was carried by fleas on rats, but no one knew this at the time. People also died of smallpox, typhus and measles in Tudor and Stuart times.

APOTHECARIES ▲

Apothecaries made pills and potions. People often took these to try and avoid painful surgery. Above is a pestle and mortar. Herbs were put into the mortar and ground into a powder or paste using the pestle. Angelica was used to help with breathing problems. Rue was used to improve people's eyesight.

WILLIAM HARVEY

William Harvey was physician to James I and Charles I. He made the most important medical discovery of the period – that the heart is a pump that makes blood flow round the body. His book about this discovery was printed in 1628.

WHO RULED THE COUNTRY?

The relationship between the monarch and Parliament was often difficult. Both sides found it hard to work together. Charles I tried ruling without Parliament. This led to civil war and his execution. Oliver Cromwell, leader of the Parliamentary army, then ruled the country. After Cromwell died, Charles I's son became King Charles II. Then came his brother James, who tried to make Britain a Catholic country again. This was so unpopular that his daughter, Mary, and her husband, William, were asked by Parliament to rule.

ELIZABETH I ▼

This portrait of Elizabeth I shows how important it was for a **ruler** to look rich and powerful. Elizabeth ordered that even pub signs had to show her looking young and beautiful!

KINGS AND QUEENS

The Crown Jewels were a symbol of the power and wealth of the monarch. The cross on the crown and the orb showed that the monarch ruled as a Christian. Rulers spent money on the things that interested them. Henry VIII bought ships and forts. Charles I bought paintings. After the execution of Charles I in 1649, the Crown Jewels were sold for £2,000. It then cost £22,000 to make a new set for Charles II!

Sceptre

St Edward's Crown

Orb

▲ EXECUTION OF CHARLES I

The **civil wars** lasted from 1642 to 1649 and killed 100,000 people. The followers of King Charles I were called the Cavaliers and they fought the Roundheads who supported Parliament. Charles was defeated and put on trial by Parliament for making war on his own people. This painting shows his **execution** on 30 January 1649. For the next eleven years, England was a **republic** ruled by Parliament. It was called 'The Commonwealth'.

COURT OF WARDS ▶

This is a painting of a Court of Wards. Committees of lawyers, like this one, did much of the routine work of government. Justices of the Peace held courts where criminals were punished. They also enforced laws about wages and prices. Local landowners decided whom to appoint as Justices of the Peace. The monarch then approved the decision.

WERE THERE ARTISTS IN TUDOR AND STUART TIMES?

Kings and Queens liked to have their own special artists. Henry VIII's official artist was Hans Holbein. He painted over 150 portraits and also made designs for buttons, buckles, costumes and armour. The architect Inigo Jones designed scenery and costumes for masques for James I (see page 37). He later planned buildings for the King. Rich people employed artists to paint portraits of their families.

PICTURES LIKE JEWELS ▼

Nicholas Hilliard was Elizabeth I's favourite artist. He painted magnificent miniature portraits like this one.

FLATTERING A KING ▶

This fine bronze statue of Charles I was made in the 1630s. Because Charles wasn't very tall, painters and sculptors showed him alone or on a horse. Standing next to someone would have shown just how short he was!

CARVING LIKE LACE ▼

This wonderful carving below is by Grinling Gibbons. He worked on St Paul's Cathedral and Hampton Court Palace. Gibbons also did carvings for churches, colleges and great houses. This carving can still be seen in Petworth House in Sussex.

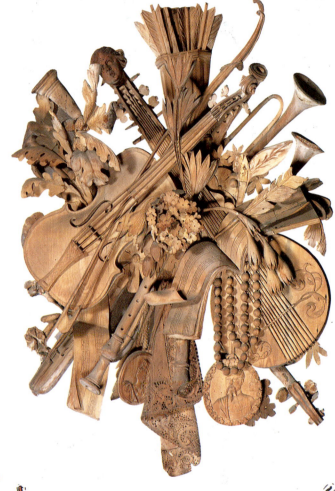

▲ THE BANQUETING HOUSE

Inigo Jones built the Palace of Whitehall in 1622 for James I. When the palace was destroyed by fire in 1698, the banqueting house (above) was the only part to survive.

Embroidered purse

Coins

FAMILIAR FACES ▲

Royal artists designed coins. Most people only ever saw their ruler on a coin.

ROYAL COLLECTOR

Charles I built up a wonderful art collection but the Puritans thought it was a huge waste of money. Many of the paintings were religious scenes painted by Catholic artists or pictures showing naked men and women. After Charles I's death, many of the paintings were sold. They can now be seen in France, Spain and Russia.

DID PEOPLE GO TO THE THEATRE?

The theatre as we know it today was a Tudor invention. Before then, plays had been acted in the streets or in the yards of inns. Having plays indoors meant actors no longer had to shout. The first theatres were in London. Sometimes actors would travel to other towns to put on plays.

ACTORS

In Tudor times all actors were men or boys. The leading actors of Shakespeare's time were James and Richard Burbage, a father and son, and Edmund Alleyne. Female actresses took to the stage after 1660. Nell Gwynn was the most famous.

STREET ENTERTAINERS ▼

This engraving shows a street entertainer with a monkey. He seems to be selling bottles of medicine as well. Jugglers and acrobats also performed at fairs and markets.

▲ WILLIAM SHAKESPEARE 1564–1616
Shakespeare was educated at a grammar school in Stratford-upon-Avon. When he came to London he worked as an actor and theatre-owner as well as writing 37 plays.

MASQUES

Masques were special shows put on for the King. They included dancing, singing and reciting verse. The costumes and scenery were wonderful. James I spent £2,000 on one masque. This was enough to pay for a warship! The architect Inigo Jones designed scenery and costumes like this one (right).

The Rose Theatre

ROSE THEATRE ▲

Above is a reconstruction of the Rose Theatre. It opened on the south bank of the Thames in 1586–7. There was no roof and if it rained the audience standing round the stage got wet. The theatre was better than an inn yard because there was less noise from the street. There were five other theatres near the Rose Theatre.

WERE THERE SCIENTISTS IN TUDOR AND STUART TIMES?

By Tudor times, scholars had learned that by studying plants and planets, they could begin to understand the natural world. New inventions included the barometer, thermometer, telescope and microscope. After 1660, the government opened the Royal Society, where new ideas were discussed and the Royal Observatory, where stars and planets were studied. An interest in science became fashionable. But the lives of ordinary people were hardly affected by science.

SUNDIAL ▲

This portable sundial belonged to Cardinal Wolsey, Henry VIII's chief minister, in the 1520s. Studying the sun, moon and stars made it possible to tell the time, navigate ships at sea and work out the calendar. Many people also believed that future events could be told from the stars and planets.

TOMPION CLOCK ▲

Thomas Tompion made the clock in the drawing above. The clock tells hours, minutes, seconds and the date. Tompion was the first English clockmaker to make small, flat clocks designed to be kept in the pocket. These were the first watches.

TELESCOPE ▶

The first telescopes were invented around 1608–9. This telescope was made around 1670 by Sir Isaac Newton. He used it to look at the stars. Newton made important discoveries about light, gravity and the planets.

Hanc Tabulam invenit & incepit Anton: Verrio, Perfecerunt Gothofredus Kneller & Jac: Thornhill Equites.

▲ SIR CHRISTOPHER WREN

This is a portrait of the famous **architect** Sir Christopher Wren. He is holding the plans of St Paul's Cathedral, which he rebuilt after the Great Fire of London in 1666.

NEW INVENTIONS

This is a list of new inventions and when they were first recorded in Britain. They may have existed much earlier if they came from other countries.

Bottle corks	1530
Artillery shells	1543
London street map	1559
Firework displays	1572
Pencil	1584
Signpost	1598
Railway	1605
Vending machine	1615
Submarine	1624
Fire engine	1632
Barometer	1648
Toothpaste	1660
Yacht	1661
Fire-hose	1674
Lamp post	1694
Steam engine	1698

Some existing inventions, like pistols, globes and spinning wheels, were improved.

Flintlock pistol

Spinning wheel　　**Globe**

DID PEOPLE GO ON LONG JOURNEYS?

Between 1500 and 1700, European sailors made great progress in shipbuilding, navigation and map-making. It became possible to trade by sea with Africa, Asia and America. But the voyages were long and dangerous. Sailors who spent weeks at sea without eating fresh fruit or vegetables could become ill. But people were willing to take risks on their voyages because of the money they could make from spices, furs, precious metals and slaves.

Francis Drake

DRAKE'S JOURNEY ▲

Francis Drake led the second voyage right round the world between 1577 and 1580. He came home a rich man and was given a **knighthood** by Elizabeth I.

This map of the world (above) was made around 1610. No one in Europe at this time knew that Australia and New Zealand existed.

HARWICH ▶

This engraving shows the Essex port of Harwich. Most ships sailed around the coasts of England moving coal or grain. It was three times faster to transport bulky goods by water than by road. It was also much cheaper.

◀ THE MAYFLOWER

This is a reconstruction of the *Mayflower*, which took the **Pilgrim Fathers** to settle in America in 1620. It was almost twice as big as the *Golden Hind* in which Drake sailed around the world. The *Mayflower* took 66 days to carry its 100 passengers across the Atlantic.

ON THE MOVE

Travel by road was dirty, tiring, slow and dangerous. On a hired horse you could travel about 30 miles a day. A royal messenger changed horses on the way and could go three times as fast.

▼ WAGONS AND HORSES

Wagons took goods and people from town to town. The journey from London to Edinburgh took one week. When Elizabeth I travelled round the country it took 400 carts to carry her baggage and **servants**!

Wagon and horses

WHAT WAS LIFE LIKE IN THE ARMY?

The civil wars of the 1640s led to the creation of an army and navy that were kept going in peacetime as well as times of war. Guns became more important in battles on land and at sea. Stone castles, armour and longbows became less important.

Henry VIII

HENRY VIII ▲

Henry VIII built up the army and the navy to protect England. He set up a royal shipyard at Deptford.

The Mary Rose

THE MARY ROSE ▲

This battleship was built for Henry VIII. When she sailed out to fight a French fleet in 1545 she capsized and sank. Only 30 of the 500 men on board survived. The wreck was found in 1967.

WELL FED

Daily rations for a Tudor soldier:
Meat – 32oz (896g)   Bread – 24oz (672g)
Cheese – 16oz (448g)   Butter – 8oz (224g)
Beer – 5 pints (2.75 litres)

DEAL CASTLE ▼

Henry VIII built 20 new **artillery** forts to protect the south-eastern coast of England from invaders. This one below is in Kent. It has openings for guns to fire in every direction.

MERCENARIES ▶

Men from poor countries like Scotland often went abroad to fight for a living. The Scots in this picture were fighting in Sweden.

WAR GAMES ▼

This photograph shows a re-enactment of a battle from the civil wars of the 1640s. Armies were made up of soldiers on horseback, soldiers firing cannons and soldiers armed with swords and guns. Up to four times as many soldiers died of disease and wounds than were killed during a battle.

GLOSSARY

AMPUTATION Cutting off a part of the body.

ANTISEPTIC A chemical used to prevent infection.

APPRENTICE A person training to learn a skilled trade or craft.

ARCHITECT A designer of buildings.

ARTILLERY Large guns such as cannons.

BAITING Chaining animals up and setting dogs to attack them.

CIVIL WAR A war between two parts of the same nation.

EXECUTION When someone is killed as a punishment.

IMPORT To buy or bring in food or other items from a foreign country.

KNIGHTHOOD An honour given by a King or Queen for a special achievement or good service.

LEECH A blood-sucking type of worm.

LIVESTOCK Animals bred for food.

MARTYR Someone who dies rather than give up what they believe.

MASQUE A special song-and-dance show performed at royal courts.

MASTER-MASON A skilled stone-cutter who managed big building projects.

MISSIONARY Someone who does religious work in a foreign country.

MONARCH A King or Queen.

NAVIGATION The art of finding your way at sea or on land.

ORB A jewelled golden ball used in a monarch's coronation ceremony.

PILGRIM FATHERS English Puritans who sailed to America and settled in Plymouth, Massachusetts in 1620.

PURITAN An English Protestant who was extremely strict about religious and moral matters.

ROSARY Special beads used by Roman Catholics to count off prayers.

RULER A person in charge of a country.

REPUBLIC A nation without a monarch, where elected representatives reign.

SCHOLAR Someone who studies.

SERVANT Someone who works for another person, looking after them or their house.

SLAVE Someone who belongs to another person and must obey them at all times.

INDEX